# **Quit Smoking**

A Manual For Temporarily Withdrawing From The Competitive Work Environment And Acquiring The Ability To Refrain From Convincing Oneself Of The Impossibility Of Resigning

**Daryl Priestley**

# TABLE OF CONTENT

Studies On Psilocybin And Addiction ..................... 1

Prevent Adverse Reactions ......................................... 6

Recognise Your Reasons For Smoking ............... 11

Why Do Individuals Begin Smoking? .................. 16

Smoking's Effects On The Heart And Blood Vessels ........................................................................... 22

Reasons For Giving Up Addiction ......................... 27

The Perils Of Cigarette Use ..................................... 33

Recognising The Need For Change: A First Step In The Healing Process ............................................ 40

Reduce How Often You Visit Bars And Clubs .. 51

Switching Out Your Habit For A New One ........ 67

Getting Ready To Give Up: Positioning Yourself For Achievement ........................................................ 73

Causes For Giving Up Smoking ............................ 86

Measures Implemented By The Iron Hands Of The Government ...................................................... 101

The Effects Of Nicotine On The Body ............... 111

Why Give Up Smoking? ........................................... 119

Easy Methods For Giving Up Smoking ............ 127

What Makes Smoking So Enjoyable For Smokers? ..................................................................... 131

Behavioural Techniques And Reversing Habits ........................................................................................ 135

Light Up And Prepare To Pay The Penalty .... 140

## Studies On Psilocybin And Addiction

Studies have been conducted on psilocybin as a possible treatment for several substance use disorders, such as addiction to alcohol, nicotine, and opioids. According to studies, this psychedelic medication can help people with an addiction become more aware of their triggers and behaviors by changing the way their brains function and reducing cravings.

Psilocybin may improve psychological well-being, allowing people to better handle stress and difficult emotions or circumstances, according to research. Cognitive-behavioral methods, including goal-setting, journaling, and guided visualization, are frequently included in psilocybin treatment sessions. These methods are helpful for those who are battling addiction.

Furthermore, research indicates that psilocybin increases activity in brain regions linked to empathy and introspection while decreasing activity in brain regions linked to fear and anxiety. This could aid individuals in comprehending their addiction and creating more constructive coping mechanisms. In the end, psilocybin may be a helpful adjunct in an all-encompassing therapy program, even though the study is still being done to understand its potential in this regard fully.

Psilocybin helps lower cravings and assist individuals in ending addiction cycles, according to recent research. For instance, a study that was published in The Pharmaceutical Journal revealed that individuals' cigarette cravings were considerably reduced over time by those who received a single dose of psilocybin. (2014, The Pharmaceutical Journal) The participants also mentioned having a higher quality of life and used nicotine replacement treatments less frequently.

How Can Psilocybin Aid In Addiction Recovery?

The results of fMRI show that psilocybin specifically interacts with serotonin 5-HT2a receptors to decrease desires. (2014, The Pharmaceutical Journal) Neuron activity reduces when psilocybin and other psychedelics trigger cerebral cortex receptors. This decline in activity diminishes the default mode network's (DMN) influence. The way we perceive ourselves in this world results from the DMN. Stated differently, introspective analysis happens within the DMN. Anxiety, OCD, PTSD, addictions, and sadness are all correlated with an overactive DMN.

Put another way, we can take a vacation from the contemplative thoughts that fuel our appetites if we can lower the activity of the DMN. An overactive DMN is the cause if you find it impossible to spend an hour without smoking because of the constant reminder that you want to smoke.

Psilocybin stops this mental monologue so those who take it won't constantly be reminded of their appetites. A fresh understanding of what matters most can emerge during this process. It's possible to drive cravings away at this epiphany.

Hormones related to the stress response, such as cortisol, are altered during psilocybin. Psilocybin stimulates the executive control network by raising cortisol levels, which then surge. Emotions and internal discourse are linked to this network. In 2017 de Veen et al.

Cortisol stops cravings and the feelings that accompany them in this way. This tiny window of time is when craving-related emotions are absent, which means they aren't fueling addictive behavior. In reality, when under the effect of psilocybin, appetites are the last thing that comes to mind.

While this is fantastic in the short term, the most amazing thing about taking psilocybin to treat smoking addiction is that, in the long run, cravings frequently don't resurface, enabling users to overcome their addictions permanently.

## Prevent Adverse Reactions

When they stop smoking, blood glucose levels often decrease. The majority of side effects that manifest during the first three days are related to diabetes. Symptoms like dizziness, headaches, and distortions in temporal perception frequently accompany this decline in blood glucose.

Anticipate the Uncomfortable

The symptoms of low oxygen levels are similar to those of low blood sugar. Low oxygen levels and blood glucose levels indicate the brain is not getting enough fuel. You cannot have enough sugar or oxygen for optimal brain function. The oxygen levels are generally higher than before when one stops smoking. But the amount of sugar in your brain is insufficient to keep it going.

The reason isn't because smoking can raise blood sugar levels. The way that drugs interact with nicotine's stimulating effect to affect blood glucose levels is more common. Smoking forces the body to burn its stores of fat and sugar. It affects your hypothalamic satiation centers and suppresses your appetite. Nicotine has a far more significant effect on sugar levels than food does.

Food can raise blood glucose levels. After you chew and swallow the food, it can take up to 20 minutes to be released into your bloodstream and, consequently, your brain, which can power it. Cigarette smoking might deplete the body's sugar reserves. Through a pharmacological interaction, this is accomplished. Sugar in food doesn't have to be eliminated from your body for years. You've done it through the drug impact of nicotine!

This explains why a lot of individuals overeat after giving up. When their blood sugar drops, they naturally go for something sweet. Even after they stop eating, they still have the same symptoms. Even though it takes them a while to consume the food, they know them. Their blood sugar levels don't increase for an additional eighteen minutes. They don't feel better right away, so they eat more. They keep eating until they start to feel better.

This is 20 minutes after their initial swallow if they wait for their blood glucose levels to increase. In twenty minutes, people might eat a lot of food. Eventually, they understand that this is the ideal quantity to feel better. This could be done often throughout the day, meaning consuming many calories and gaining weight.

When you quit smoking, your body will experience a loss. It has yet to operate normally for a long time, so it won't know how. After the third day, your body will start to adjust, and you will no longer need sugar. By consuming less, your body will develop better blood glucose regulation skills.

You may need to adjust your eating habits to make them more reliable. Regular is more akin to what it was before you were given an aging injection than it is to what it was before you started smoking. Despite smoking, some people can go to the evening without eating. If they attempt the same thing as former smokers, they will suffer from low blood sugar adverse effects.

They were previously unique for pragmatic reasons, but they are manageable currently. They may need to spread their meal consumption to ensure they receive the necessary blood glucose dosages throughout the day, but they may only sometimes need to eat more.

After the fourth day, if you follow a regular diet, your body should be able to flush out any stored sugar, so this shouldn't be required.

Speaking with your doctor if your blood glucose issues persist after day 3 is a good idea. You may also think about receiving dietary counseling. If you want your body to maintain permanent control over the quantity of sugar (glucose) in your brain, put down that next cigarette.

# Recognise Your Reasons For Smoking

Determining your smoking motivation can be a difficult and very personal process. Smoking is a behavior that can have different meanings for different people. To understand the underlying causes of smoking, one must be willing to look within and analyze their thoughts, feelings, and habits. To help you understand why you smoke, follow these steps:

Introspection: To start, set up a calm, cozy area where you can think clearly and independently about your smoking habits. Try to explore your feelings and thoughts related to smoking by asking yourself why you smoke. Think about the places and times you smoke, the feelings you get from it, and any trends or triggers that are connected to your smoking habit.

Determine Triggers: Observe the circumstances or occurrences that make you want to grab a cigarette. Physical triggers include things like waking up in the morning or finishing a meal; emotional triggers include things like stress, boredom, or anxiety; and social triggers include things like being around friends who smoke. Understanding your triggers will help you understand the underlying reasons behind your smoking habit.

Emotional Intelligence: Smoking is frequently used as a coping strategy for challenging emotions. It can offer momentary solace from tension, worry, or melancholy. Think about whether smoking makes you feel more at ease, self-assured, or able to block off specific feelings. Make a note of any emotional patterns that you link with smoking and look into more healthful ways to express your emotions.

Habitual Associations: Smoking can cause deeply rooted behaviors that are difficult to break into our everyday lives. Look at the events or activities that you instantly associate with smoking. For instance, smoking after meals or during work breaks might be more of a habit than a particular need. Understanding these connections can assist you in creating non-smoking substitute practices.

Societal Factors: Consider how societal factors have influenced your smoking behavior. Since smoking is frequently a social activity, peer pressure and the need to fit in can be major motivators for smoking. Think about the people you usually smoke with and how their influence affects your smoking habits.

Gaining insight into how social dynamics influence your smoking decisions will help you become more self-reliant.

Early Life Events and Conditioning: Examine any programming or experiences from your early years that might have shaped your attitude towards smoking. For instance, growing up in a home where smoking was common or witnessing someone smoke as a stress reliever may have influenced your belief that smoking is a required or normal behavior. Understanding these effects can assist you in reframing and challenging your smoking-related beliefs.

Alternate Coping Strategies: After determining the underlying demands that led to your smoking habit, think about using alternate coping techniques to meet those needs. If you smoke, for instance, try better methods of reducing stress, such as working out, practicing meditation, or speaking with a confidant. If you smoke as a form of boredom relief, look for interesting pastimes or pursuits to satisfy that need.

Seek Assistance: It can be difficult to understand why you smoke and to make the necessary changes to your smoking habit on your own. Joining support groups or counseling sessions devoted to quitting smoking could be a good idea.

Track Development: Keep track of your progress and assess how it affects your smoking behavior as you make adjustments and take up new coping mechanisms. Keep track of any alterations in your emotional state, triggers, or desires. Since quitting smoking is frequently a prolonged process, acknowledge little triumphs and learn from losses.

## Why Do Individuals Begin Smoking?

It's a serious question, especially in light of the widespread advertising on TV, radio, and in school textbooks that highlight the negative effects of smoking cigarettes. It seems that the majority of people begin smoking in their teens and develop an addiction by the time they reach adulthood. Trying to appear more adult is one of the main motivations for someone starting to smoke cigarettes. They may also be experimenting or trying to follow in the footsteps of their peers. Adolescents who live with elderly smokers are at a higher risk of becoming smokers themselves. They will smoke to appear older, especially if they are under social pressure to do so. Experimenting with smoking has always been motivated by a desire to do something forbidden. Despite the fact that it is illegal for anyone under the age of eighteen to smoke in the majority of countries on Earth, the idea of smoking remains alluring to young people. It's exactly the same thing that occurs when you want to try something because you think it sounds interesting, but your parent says you're not allowed to.

Adults, however, smoke for a variety of reasons. To start, individuals frequently experience high levels of stress and strain in their lives, particularly as a result of both personal and financial challenges. It's possible that they are employed in a position where their pay is insufficient to support the lifestyle they have always desired. Adults may also be struggling with substance addiction or be in a toxic relationship. It has been repeatedly demonstrated that all of these stressors enhance cigarette smoking as people attempt to de-stress.

These are some of the main additional reasons why individuals smoke, regardless of age.

Influences of the Media

Similar to advertising, the media's influence is immense. The way that viewers make decisions can be greatly influenced by the media. This is a daily occurrence for both haircuts and popular clothes labels. In actuality, smoking in the media can affect viewers in the same way that their favorite actress's wardrobe does. Recent studies have shown that when young people observe a popular figure or character they look up to smoking, they are more likely to start smoking themselves. People often believe it to be fashionable, socially acceptable, and, moreover, trendy. Health organizations and anti-smoking campaigns have been pushing hard to lower onscreen smoking lately.

The public's perception of smoking as socially acceptable is intended to be altered by this.

## DNA

Medical research in the realm of genetics is beginning to imply that addictions may have a hereditary component, even though there isn't any conclusive evidence yet. These studies look at how certain people can be more prone to smoking addiction than others due to genetic vulnerability to specific health and sociocultural conditions, even though they don't specifically focus on a single gene that is linked to smoking.

## Consuming False Information

The media has been heavily promoting tobacco products lately. The majority of nations have tight regulations on this kind of advertising, yet the impacts of persistently spreading false information about tobacco continue to be a major cause of new smoking instances.

## Mode of taking risks

As improbable as it may sound, youths who lean towards risk-taking behavior may find these constraints to be alluring. As it is, there's a certain excitement associated with breaching the law. When you take into account that certain kids are likely to disobey regulations set by their communities, schools, and parents, it makes sense that the "risk-taking mode" is a major contributing factor to youth smoking.

## Observe the Smoke

Frequently, one can hear a smoker pull a fast one-liner from their smoking habits, such as "I love to watch the smoke." Indeed, smoke has numerous symbolic implications in both mythology and religion. There is something about its ethereal allure that elicits feelings in support of smoking. For this reason, people frequently remark that "smoke is fascinating." Smokers enjoy unwinding by just sitting back and letting the puffs disperse into thin air.

Anyone who ever lights up has the potential to develop a nicotine addiction. Studies show that the adolescent years are when people are most prone to develop a smoking addiction. Thus, in order to prevent their children from taking up smoking, parents should keep a close eye on them throughout this time.

# Smoking's Effects On The Heart And Blood Vessels

Smoking is a preventable cause of death that takes 5 million lives each year around the world. While millions of dollars are spent searching for disease cures, many individuals are unable to give up smoking, enhance their health, or save money.

Raise the Chance of Getting Atherosclerosis

Smokers' blood levels of fibrinogen, a glycoprotein that promotes blood clot formation, are higher in cigarette smokers. Additionally, their platelet counts are higher, which thickens the blood.

Smoking also lowers your good HDL cholesterol levels while significantly increasing your bad cholesterol or LDL cholesterol.

Smoking produces chemicals that irritate your blood vessels, causing inflammation that damages and stiffens the walls of your blood vessels. Another common cause of heart attacks and strokes is inflammation.

Any of the aforementioned factors alone may be problematic, but when they combine, the chance of developing atherosclerosis increases.

Heart Attack

Your heart and blood vessels react instantly to each cigarette you inhale. When you inhale, your heart rate quickens within a minute and can rise by as much as 30% in ten minutes.

Your blood vessels narrow as a result of smoking, which raises blood pressure and puts stress on the heart. Because carbon monoxide binds to hemoglobin so readily, blood's capacity to carry oxygen to all body tissues is negatively impacted.

Your heart beats more quickly and elevates blood pressure in an attempt to overcome the difficulty it is having pumping oxygen to other parts of your body.

Every cigarette you smoke has an impact on your coronary health because cigarettes contain chemicals that harm the lining of your heart's arteries.

Increased Risk of Death from Ruptured Aneurysm

The artery wall ballooning is called an aneurysm. A smoker is more likely to die from a ruptured aneurysm due to this swelling's increased propensity to clot and burst.

A ruptured aneurysm may occur without any symptoms or warning signs, and it can be fatal. It can result in a stroke if it's not fatal.

Risk of Peripheral Vascular Disease (PVD) Incurred

Smokers who ignore the first signs of clogged veins in their legs or feet run the risk of developing gangrene. Anyone who has already had surgery for PVD should most likely anticipate a recurrence of the illness. Regrettably, it may result in death or amputation.

One type of PVD that affects heavy smokers is called thromboangiitisobliterans, a rare condition. It begins with a small blood vessel inflammatory condition that progresses to an artery blockage. Studies reveal that the majority of those afflicted with this illness need multiple amputations and that very few are able to stop gangrene from developing.

Give Up Smoking Right Away

If one quits smoking, they can prevent these.

Your chance of passing away from heart disease will be identical to that of a non-smoker after ten years of not smoking. It will be as though you never smoked at all, so giving up now is worthwhile for your long-term health.

## Reasons For Giving Up Addiction

Motivation to overcome addiction is a crucial component of the healing process. The following are some typical excuses people give for kicking an addiction:

Health issues: Addiction can have detrimental impacts on both mental and physical health, from heightened disease risk to compromised cognitive performance. The desire to get healthier might be the main driver behind some people's decision to stop using drugs.

Relationship problems: Addiction can cause social isolation and loneliness as well as strain relationships with friends, family, and romantic partners. Restoring damaged connections and establishing new ones can be a strong recovery motivator for people who value their relationships.

Legal issues: Addiction-related behaviors or substance abuse can lead to legal issues like fines, jail time, or arrest.

The main driving force behind some people's addiction recovery may be their desire to avoid these repercussions.

Concerns about finances: Addiction can be expensive, both in terms of the money spent on drugs or alcohol and the harm it can do to one's ability to perform at work or earn a living. One of the strongest incentives for recovery may be the wish to increase financial stability or prevent financial disaster.

Personal development: Addiction can keep people from following their passions or reaching their own goals. A major driving force behind some people's decision to overcome addiction may be their desire to develop personally and realize their full potential.

Spirituality: Addiction may be at odds with a person's spiritual or religious beliefs for some people. Recovery can be greatly aided by the desire to live in accordance with one's spiritual values and beliefs.

In the end, the reasons for kicking an addiction differ from person to person and can evolve over time. It's critical that people recognize their own reasons for wanting to recover and that they draw strength and inspiration from these reasons as they move through the process.

## The advantages of kicking an addiction

There are many advantages to giving up addiction, including improved personal and professional relationships, mental and physical health, and more. The following are some of the main advantages of beating addiction:

Better physical health: Giving up an addiction can enhance general well-being, lower the risk of illness, and improve physical health.

Improved mental health: Giving up addiction can enhance mental well-being, lessen the signs of mental illness, and enhance one's general quality of life.

Better relationships: Addiction can cause tension in friendships, family, and romantic relationships, which can result in social exclusion and hostility. Giving up addiction can aid in mending strained bonds between people and fostering new ones founded on respect and trust.

Stability in finances: Addiction can be costly, which can result in instability and financial issues. Reducing spending on drugs and alcohol, enhancing productivity at work, and raising earning potential are all ways that addiction recovery can contribute to greater financial stability.

Enhanced self-worth: Addiction can cause feelings of guilt, shame, and low self-worth by undermining confidence and self-esteem. Giving up an addiction can boost confidence and self-worth, which can lead to

How to find your own inner drive to give up

Although it can be difficult, finding the motivation to stop an addiction is necessary to succeed in recovery. Here are some potential helpful strategies:

Determine the Causes of Your Quit: Give your reasons for wanting to quit some thought. Put them in writing, being as detailed as you can. These could be for a variety of reasons, such as wanting to enhance your general quality of life, financial concerns, interpersonal relationships, or health issues.

See the Advantages: Consider how much better your life will be after you give up. Imagine the benefits of quitting, such as better health, more energy, stronger relationships, and a stronger sense of self-worth.

Seek Assistance: Addiction can be difficult to overcome on your own. Seek out assistance from loved ones, close friends, or a qualified counselor who can guide you through the process. Having a support system and someone with whom to confide in one another can help sustain motivation.

Establish Objectives: Having measurable, defined goals will help you stay motivated to stop. Put your goals down in writing and create a strategy to reach them. This can entail making a quit date, going to support groups, or getting help from a professional.

Keep Your Attention in the Here and Now: It's simple to become paralyzed by the thought of giving up addiction permanently. Rather, live in the now and deal with each day as it comes. Enjoy every little accomplishment along the road, and be forgiving of yourself when mistakes are made. Keep in mind that recovery is a process that requires patience and hard work.

## The Perils Of Cigarette Use

Before anything else, there are a lot of risks associated with smoking for you personally. Your body is the first thing that smoking destroys. The hazards that smoking poses to the body include the following:

The respiratory system is affected by the harmful substances in cigarettes, which cause damage to your lungs the moment you inhale smoke. Because they are exposed to pneumonia, bronchitis, asthma, coughing, and wheezing, it also affects those in your immediate vicinity.

Long-term smoking causes a host of issues, and when combined with an increased risk of infection, it puts smokers at risk for developing chronic lung conditions that are irreversible. Among these prerequisites are the following:

COPD stands for chronic obstructive pulmonary disease.

Prolonged bronchitis

inflammation of the lung's respiratory tube lining

Cancer of the lung

Asthma

Whistling and Coughing

Pneumonia and Asthma

When the lungs and airways heal, quitting smoking may result in congestion and discomfort in the respiratory system. Mucus production has increased, which indicates that your respiratory system is nearing recovery.

If this continues for an extended period of time, the blood vessels are harmed, and the flow is narrowed, leading to peripheral artery diseases. In addition, smoking increases blood pressure, weakens blood vessel walls, and promotes blood clots, all of which increase the risk of stroke. Smoking exposes others to secondhand smoke and poses the same risk to nonsmokers as it does to smokers, despite your belief that it only affects you.

Central Nervous System (CNS): Nicotine, a drug that affects mood, is one of tobacco's active ingredients. It provides you with a temporary boost in energy and enters the brain in a matter of seconds. You'll experience fatigue and a craving for more nicotine as the effects wear off. Because nicotine is habit-forming and addictive, quitting smoking is more difficult for smokers. Withdrawing from nicotine damages the brain's cognitive area, causing agitation, depression, and anxiety. You will be able to manage all of it if you follow the advice in that book, even though it also occasionally causes headaches and insomnia.

The Integumentary System, which includes the skin, hair, and nails, is impacted by smoking in addition to the internal organs. Smoking tobacco alters the composition of the skin and raises the risk of squamous cell carcinoma, a type of skin cancer. Additionally, it raises the risk of toenail and finger fungal infections. It also causes hair loss and turns the hair grey or bald.

Reproductive System: Nicotine has an impact on both men's and women's blood flow to the genital regions. Because there is less lubrication, men's sexual performance is reduced, which leads to sexual dissatisfaction and the inability to experience an orgasm. In addition, smoking reduces the amount of sex hormones in both males and females, which in turn causes a decrease in sexual desire in both.

Digestive system: Smoking raises the risk of larynx, pancreatic, throat, esophageal, and mouth cancers; this effect extends to nonsmokers as well. Additionally, smoking increases your risk of insulin resistance, type 2 diabetes, and stroke.

Your sense of taste and smell are affected by smoking. Nicotine decreases taste sensitivity by influencing the taste buds in the oral cavity.

Smoking confines you to a life of struggle against repressed withdrawal symptoms.

It leads you right back into the things (depression and anxiety) you're running away from. Smokers' depression is caused by nicotine, which enters the body with each cigarette smoked and prevents the body from producing the "joy hormones," which are thought to be responsible for an individual's emotional state.

Your physical appearance is negatively impacted (unpleasant odor, bad skin structure, yellow teeth, etc.). The toxic substances contained in the smoke of cigarettes, together with nicotine, contribute to the destruction of collagen fibers of the skin.

It reduces your energy level and your ability to perform physical exercise. Shortness of breath, nausea, decreased stamina, increased blood pressure, rapid heartbeat - this is what you can experience after one cigarette smoked two hours before entering a sports club. So to achieve good results and progress for the smoker is much more difficult than for a person who is free from this habit (provided that both have a similar level of physical fitness).

It costs you finances. Just make an average calculation of how much smoking costs you in the year. Perhaps you can go to Europe on a trip with that money, right?

# Recognising The Need For Change: A First Step In The Healing Process

I discovered a couple of terms in the Cambridge dictionary that best described the word "acknowledge" when searching for it in the dictionary. To acknowledge something is to accept, acknowledge, or recognize it as true or real. These phrases, in my opinion, capture my intentions for this the best. Addiction in any form must first be acknowledged, acknowledged, and accepted as a need for change.

Let's examine these words in more detail. To admit is to enter a guilty plea for a course. It implies that in order to receive aid, you must acknowledge your need for it and be prepared to make every effort to obtain it. And I promise that this book in your hands has all the assistance you require. Accepting is another word for acknowledgment, and it seems to suggest that you accept the diagnosis that this book is about to give you. A doctor is a professional with the exclusive duty of identifying the different problems pertaining to a man's health; nevertheless, before a person finds a doctor, they must acknowledge the necessity of seeing a doctor.

These three words—accepting, acknowledging, and realizing that you are hooked and that you need help—are the keys to breaking free from addiction. Patients come to the doctor for these three reasons, and the physician can treat them when they acknowledge that their bodies don't work properly in addition to providing a diagnosis. This is where the book starts. How can I tell if I have an addiction? When should I declare my addiction? How can I kick an addiction?

Addiction is the inability to give up a substance or behavior, even when doing so may be harmful to one's physical or mental health.

The word "addiction" refers to more than just alcohol or drug addiction. An inability to stop doing certain things, including eating, working, or gambling, is another sign of some addictions. Medication use can lead to the development of addiction, a chronic disorder. In actuality, abuse of opioids—particularly fentanyl produced illegally—caused close to 50,000 deaths in the US alone in 2019.

Addicts use drugs or engage in obsessive behaviours that they frequently carry out in spite of unfavourable outcomes." Though not everyone starts doing drugs or other activities of their own volition, many do. However, addiction has the power to take over and impede self-control.

An individual is considered addicted if any of the following starts to occur in their life.

And when you can take more before experiencing any effects at all. The effects of the medicine wear off, and you feel weird. You can be sweaty, dizzy, sad, queasy, or experiencing headaches. You might also be hungry or fatigued. In extreme situations, you can experience confusion, convulsions, or fever.

Another clue is if the person is continually trying to stop using the substance but is unable to do so on their own, even with their best efforts. You keep using it despite the fact that it's having a bad impact on your life and getting in the way of things like arguments with friends, family, coworkers, or the law.

It takes a great deal of courage and introspection to recognize the need for change. It means accepting reality as it is, no matter how unpleasant, and realizing that in order to regain control and find a path to recovery, a change is necessary. It means acknowledging the negative effects addiction has had on their relationships, general well-being, and physical and mental health. This is a show of strength—the courage to face our weaknesses and the will to work towards a brighter future—rather than an admission of weakness.

Addressing our denial and the harsh reality that our addiction has grown out of hand is the first step toward making a change. Before gaining freedom, a guy must acknowledge that his addiction has taken control of his life.

At this time, a person realizes that their ability to grow personally, be happy, and accomplish their goals is being hampered by substance abuse or obsessive behavior. This realization of oneself is a turning point that opens doors to transformation and creates the foundation for a life in recovery.

Acknowledging the necessity for change is an ongoing process rather than an isolated incident. It requires that the person continually renew their commitment to their recovery, particularly in the face of temptation or misfortune. It acts as a reminder that change is challenging and that obstacles may arise along the way. But once the person acknowledges that something needs to change, they can use their inner strength and resolve to go beyond obstacles and keep going towards recovery.

Why Give Up Smoking at All?

There are a plethora of diverse rationales or incentives for giving up smoking.

Well-being

The most common one has to do with health. Cigarette smoking is unhealthy. Furthermore, smoking's side effects are extremely unpleasant, even in situations where they are not necessarily lethal. A person's total quality of life is severely impacted by conditions like hypertension, heart disease, kidney disease, halitosis (poor breath), infertility in women, and impotence in males.

Cash

In this society, money can be a powerful motivator for virtually everything, and smoking is no exception. Money can seem more essential than health at times, especially to certain individuals.

After all, money is what keeps the world turning, and smoking is undoubtedly a costly habit. We are talking about the purchase of tobacco, which is an expensive endeavor in and of itself; we are not even taking into account the potential costs of medical treatments in the event of health issues.

As the most common type of tobacco, a pack of cigarettes usually costs $5 to $10 in the USA. Prices in Western Europe are similar or occasionally slightly more, and since the average smoker smokes about one pack a day, that adds up to $150 or $300 per month. Only for purchasing cigarettes

Momentum

Another compelling argument for giving up smoking may be time. Given that time is arguably the most valuable resource we possess, it would seem futile to lose a few hours each day to smoking or to reduce the total number of days one has due to smoking, doesn't it? If you have any doubts about the veracity of the statement, it truly is hours.

The average smoker wastes around 30 full days – a month of life – smoking 20 cigarettes a day, each of which lasts for 5 to 7 minutes. This means that the daily total for the act of smoking is roughly 2 hours! Once more, that is time dedicated solely to smoking!

Not even taken into consideration are other smoking-related rituals, including purchasing tobacco goods, cleaning your teeth or hands after smoking, walking to a designated smoking location, and so forth. The daily total would likely be closer to three hours if they were.

An inquiry from a third-party

A common motivation for quitting smoking is receiving a request—or even a demand—from another person. A medical professional. A companion. An absolute stranger. From an authority figure, such as the government or the landlord of a flat one is renting. Or a spouse!

At first glance, this desire to stop smoking doesn't seem all that great, does it? However, if you slightly alter it to show the true motivations behind it, it begins to make sense. Love, honor, and sincerity. These are the actual justifications for persuading someone to give up smoking at another person's request.

unpleasant smell

Another very common reason to give up smoking is the scent. If you smoke, you are aware that smoking leaves an unpleasant aftertaste in your mouth, but it also has longer-lasting and wider effects. It stains skin, hair, clothes, and even homes.

If smokers are not bothered by the stench, then it may not be such a bad thing; the issue is that others are frequently bothered by the stench. Smoking can turn someone into a social outcast. Someone whom others despise.Someone who is not liked by other people.Someone that other people don't want.Someone that other people shun.

Other

Of fact, there are many more reasons, but it would be useless to enumerate them all. It really doesn't matter too much why you want to continue smoking. All that matters is that you have one and that it is legitimate. True for you.

## Reduce How Often You Visit Bars And Clubs

Do you want to cut back on how often you drink alcohol and eventually give it up entirely? Well, give up frequenting bars. Saying that you have the self-control to avoid alcohol while in a bar is a foolish statement because the main function of bars is "to socialise."

You're not correct. Bars exist primarily to serve drinks. The beverages are on the table before the socializing begins. This being the case, you will naturally feel compelled to get one. Because of "profits," there is a purposefully constructed drinking atmosphere at bars and clubs.

It might be extremely difficult, if not completely impossible, to resist purchasing a drink given the low, gloomy lighting, the lingering scent of alcohol mixed with cologne and perfume, and the seductive, carefree atmosphere that permeates the entire area. Therefore, if you want to succeed in your battle against alcohol, it's essential to stay away from them completely.

For the sake of argument, what if you were invited to a happy hour or other social gathering in a bar with your boss and coworkers? Try ordering a club soda or another non-alcoholic beverage if that's the case.

Lime juice is sometimes a good choice if you're trying to avoid looking too square while sipping a club soda. However, some people find it to be a bit too sweet. Order a treat from the food menu if the bar serves it, so you may pretend to be indulging when you're not.

Select a pub that offers much more than simply alcohol when you get there. For example, you can find bocce balls or pool tables at many bars. These kinds of bars/places are great since it's not all about how much alcohol you're swallowing. It will be simpler to cut back on alcohol or not drink at all.

Having said all of this, you will also need to exercise caution with other things. First, steer clear of the overt ways to boost alcohol consumption, such as advertisements for alcohol, happy hour specials, oversized shot glasses, and pitchers that increase alcohol intake quickly.

Remember that bartenders can also subtly influence you through unsubtle flirtation, strategic intimacy, and offering to buy you drinks or shots on the house in order to get you to buy alcohol.

Bartenders are quite cunning when it comes to using music and subtle gestures to get customers to drink more. The other patrons will also contribute to the libation-heavy mood by kissing, singing, calling for toasts, and engaging in close dancing. Being aware of these things and being cautious to avoid getting drawn into the vortex would be helpful.

This does not, however, imply that you should cower in a corner or remain rigid and unresponsive. Purchasing a single drink and sipping it continuously while moving about and mingling with the people around you is a useful tactic. You may always refer to your unfinished drink to make others think you're drinking if they offer to buy you a drink.

The following basic block is similarly related to the one discussed here; the subsequent Step examines participating in non-alcoholic activities.

So, do you consider yourself to be a smoker now? It may cause you to eat less, or it may provide you with stress relief. You may even be able to control your desire for alcohol and other addictive substances by quitting smoking. You may not enjoy smoking for a variety of reasons.

It could be a good idea to assess your readiness for this significant life transition before deciding to break this behavior. You should actually build a few lists and consider what you put on them before doing that.

Why am I such a big fan of smoking?

"What so great about smoking?" is the title of one of the first lists you should make before determining whether or not you are truly ready to give up smoking. You should mention all the reasons you enjoy smoking in this list. It may sound paradoxical, but you'll discover that the negative aspects of smoking will almost certainly outweigh the positive aspects.

By doing this, you'll become more aware of what has to be done and whether you're ready to accomplish it. It will also inspire you to consider how you're going to break this habit that you detest so much on a subconscious level, which will help you become more motivated.

You can really get things going with this list!

Why do I detest smoking?

It would also be wise for you to take into account all of the reasons you detest smoking. The odor that accompanies you everywhere, terrible breath, the amount of money you have to spend, damaged teeth and lungs, a weakened immune system, and a host of other issues might all fall under this category. You will have more than enough motivation to want to stop smoking when you have this big list of things about yourself that you dislike because you smoke.

A lot of the things you put on this list may impact more people than just you and have more than one meaning. For instance, you might notice that your foul breath makes your partner less likely to kiss you, or you might notice that you're the one who always gets sick in the family because of the significant and detrimental effects smoking may be having on your immune system. Not to mention that loud, embarrassing smoker's cough you may be showing off in public, in your classrooms, at church, or at parties and company gatherings.

This list has a plethora of items that could significantly influence your decision to quit smoking.

What would occur if I gave up smoking?

Now, combine the two lists you completed before with this one, and make a list of several activities you could do if you stopped smoking. This can involve a number of things, such as being able to play with your kids for longer periods of time and not having to walk outside in the cold to smoke, among many other things.

For most people, this list will be the make-or-break factor. It will assist you in making the ultimate decision about whether you want to spend the rest of your life squandering money on cigarettes or spending the rest of your days leading."

What's the deal?

As I've previously stated, compiling all three of these lists will undoubtedly assist you in making the best choice for yourself. They will also encourage and motivate you to make the decision. After creating these lists, if you still feel unprepared to give up smoking, put this book down and give it another go when you're certain you're ready for the endeavor. It could be a huge waste of time and energy to give up if you're not ready.

But after looking over your lists, you may decide that you're ready to overcome this, that you're ready to change into the person you want to be, that you want to be more energetic, and that you want to feel better about yourself. Making a list and reflecting on what might have been and what might be in the future can lead to a lot of positive things.


Giving up cigarettes is not just about reliance for some people.

In fact, many people have developed the bad habit of lighting up as soon as they experience stress or problems in their lives. Some people simply have the habit of needing a smoke as soon as they finish their meal.

Whatever the cause, the habit has the potential to be just as addictive as actual nicotine. Not only must you remove the reliance, but you also need to learn how to break the habit.

You might want to try a replacement type of therapy if you find that you are missing out on the hand-to-mouth action or habit that you were engaging in when you were smoking. This therapy will allow you to have the same hand-to-mouth activity without the assistance of cigarettes.

Some people bring carrot sticks as a healthful way to enjoy hand-to-mouth contact without smoking. Some may substitute sugar-free candies for cigarettes. You will succeed in stopping cigarettes by using whatever means necessary to reduce the habit.

Stop Smoking Aids in Four.

There are several items available to help those who wish to stop smoking cigarettes, even if they don't think they have the self-control to do so.

The categories range from over-the-counter products to pharmaceuticals with a guarantee of efficacy. These days, there are more products available to help people give up than there are different brands of cigarettes.

All you need to do is walk into any type of store, and you'll find a plethora of resources to help people give up smoking cigarettes. Try conducting an online search; you will find an abundance of products designed specifically to help you quit smoking.

Once you've made the decision to give up smoking and you want to use assistance to help you do so, you should research the various methods accessible to you in order to gain an understanding of what is available and how they work.

Since there are many different brands, I will concentrate on sharing with you only the methods, benefits and drawbacks of each type of assistance.

It makes little sense to dive into brand names because that is usually a matter of preference and may also depend on budget.

While certain brand names may cost more than others, they provide the same support to individuals who wish to stop smoking cigarettes.

If you are confined to your home, you can browse any of the online bookstores, which will provide a selection of books on quitting smoking. It will be possible for you to get e-books such as this one that will help you give up smoking.

Many of these books are quite beneficial when it comes to quitting smoking. Some people find that it could be simpler to give up after reading about a subject.

## WHY IT'S TOUGH TO QUIT

Understanding how to use pain and pleasure rather than letting them use you is the key to success. You have control over your life if you take that action. If not, you are at the mercy of life.
-- Anthony Robbins

Amputations, repeated heart attacks, circulatory disorders leading to cancer, emphysema, and other fatal and incapacitating illnesses have all been reported by some smokers.

Even though they are completely aware that smoking is ruining their lives, they still smoke. Any reasonable person, smoker or not, has the right to ask, "why?" After all that, how in the world could these people have kept smoking?

Such a complicated question has a really easy solution.

Cigarette smoking is a psychological habit as well as a physical addiction. Nicotine, a highly addictive substance, is an ingredient in cigarettes. Nicotine is highly addictive and can provide a momentary sense of relaxation and/or stress reduction the faster it reaches your brain.

When you stop getting your daily nicotine dose, you'll want to smoke another cigarette. As a result of nicotine's "pleasant feeling" influence on your brain, you might have developed a habit of smoking to help you deal with stress, anxiety, despair, rage, or even loneliness.

Simultaneously, smoking takes on significant importance in your life. You associate certain individuals, feelings, and activities with smoking. Almost everything you do from the moment you wake up until you go to bed is included in these activities.

For instance, you might smoke your first cigarette just after eating or as soon as you wake up in the morning. You light up before going to bed at night or during a break from work or school. Maybe you interact with smokers on a regular basis since friends, family, and coworkers are part of your social circle.

Finding strategies to break the habit is just as important as quitting the addiction if you want to make a complete recovery.

# Switching Out Your Habit For A New One

Everybody is a creature of habit. There are those among us who follow stricter routines, such as "I wear my slippers every Friday at eight o'clock... in November." Some people have less structure—"I put on my slippers whenever I want." You are aware of your smoking habits and how dependent you are on cigarettes.

You'll have to use fire to combat fire in either case. Make new, healthy habits to replace your old ones.

You might have smoked for many years, even decades. You seem to have an etched trail in your brain from these years, leaving a lasting psychological mark. You will need to replace your cigarette addiction with something you are enthusiastic about and something you know you can live with.

This is where understanding your smoking habits and the side effects is essential to your success.

Food Avoidance: Especially during the first month or two, you'll need to find a way to fill the hole left by smoking if you're trying to avoid overindulging. Some people chew gum, while others use sugar-free candies. A relative of mine switched to air-popped popcorn, but I found that beef jerky was the finest option.

Hand-to-mouth communication: This element can be your largest obstacle; it certainly was mine. So make sure you're ready for this switch by being "armed." I would consume things slowly and avoid gaining weight by using items that required time to digest, such as jerky or unsalted sunflower seeds. My main concern was to overcome the want for cigarettes, not to consider healthy eating alternatives. Make careful to first discuss any changes to your diet with your physician.

Boredom: When nothing interesting is happening, smoking tends to fill the void. Simply shifting to a different room seemed to help. Leaving my favorite smoking location broke the "flow" of my cigarettes. You can now keep your smartphone ready to use for other activities. You may download a tonne of entertaining and informative phone apps to make coping with boredom (wherever you are) much simpler and more productive.

It's advisable to pick up a hobby, such as painting, knitting, or playing an instrument (don't laugh). These are a few instances of substitution that are constructive. Needless to say, knitting is not for the lint-phobic.

Discover who you are.

Pick up that passion you've been putting off for a while and join an online community about it. I use free software on my phone that helps me study Japanese anytime I have to wait for something. It's the ideal stand-in for those slumps that could jeopardize your ability to stop successfully.

You're probably thinking desperately, "Knitting and phone apps aren't a cigarette," regardless of anything I say or recommend. I'm going to crave my smoke. Knitting needles won't have the same flavor or sensation as cigarettes. And you'll continue to talk with useless gibberish. You're correct, though; this is absurd reasoning. Please give your substitute a serious attempt.

It is seriously necessary for you to end this unhealthy relationship. Chew on straws if that's what it takes to stop.

Please be patient with me; we will soon get to the point of the how-to. As with anything in life, preparation is a necessary step in the process.

Finding the Things That Will Motivate You to Quit

It is imperative that you thoroughly study and comprehend this section before moving on to five's actual quitting methods.

Whether it's money, family, youth, beauty, or health, everyone has something they cherish. We all have fears, and we are aware of which of these things drives us, just like our ideals. When it comes to quitting smoking, you'll need to make the most of your most cherished and feared aspects.

Avoid approaching the process of breaking your addiction with the fear that, as you might have in the past, you'll give in and start smoking.

Have confidence in yourself.

NOTE: You'll need total, round-the-clock access to the notes I offer below, so if you don't have a cell phone, I suggest you invest in a few index cards to save your motivators.

## Getting Ready To Give Up: Positioning Yourself For Achievement

It can be difficult to stop smoking, but it is possible to do so successfully if you are prepared. Assessing motivation, locating resources for assistance, looking at triggers, and picking up new behavioral techniques should all be part of the preparation process.

Assess your reasons for wanting to stop first. Think about your motivation for quitting, your desired outcomes, and the benefits you stand to gain. To assist you in staying motivated throughout the process, put these reasons in writing. There isn't a "right" solution, but you can take back control of your life and your habits by knowing why you want to stop and by making meaningful goals.

Having a support network is crucial to a successful quit. Seek guidance and support from loved ones, friends, support groups, individual counseling, and other available resources. Assure yourself that you have all the help you require to succeed and that you are not traveling alone.

Analyze your own triggers and develop coping mechanisms. Smoking frequently develops into a conditioned, automatic reaction to particular events and feelings. Planning alternate coping mechanisms can be facilitated by being aware of high-risk circumstances and the factors that lead to them. Deep breathing exercises and other approaches for diversion are examples of coping mechanisms.

Finally, develop behavioral and cognitive techniques to assist you in successfully stopping by fortifying your willpower.

Instead of using mindfulness practices as a way to divert your attention, try focusing on relaxing and being in the present moment by doing yoga and meditation. You can stay motivated by actively participating in the quitting process by tracking your progress and creating daily objectives.

You are putting yourself in a successful smoking cessation position by examining your reasons for stopping, encircling yourself with people who support you, controlling personal triggers, and learning new skills. You can succeed in quitting smoking if you put in the necessary planning and grit. Wishing you luck!

Finding Your "Why": Inspiration for Transformation

Knowing why you want to stop smoking is crucial when thinking about doing so. Everybody has a different reason for wanting to stop, and the secret to a successful quit attempt may be knowing why it matters to them personally. It's crucial to recognize both internal and external motivators while speculating on this reason.

Internal motivators are those that originate from the inside and can provide you with the willpower and fortitude necessary to effect long-term change. This could be a desire to make a wise, life-altering choice, feel better, or have more energy. This type of drive is frequently the strongest and can originate from the heart.

The people and things outside of you that might keep you moving in the direction of achievement are known as external motivators. This could be the support of close friends or family members, as well as monetary incentives like discounts on medical expenses or prizes for abstaining from smoking.

It might also be beneficial for you to keep in mind that smoking is associated with specific social contexts. People are frequently more likely to smoke when they are with friends, in stressful conditions, or in circumstances where cravings could arise. When attempting to prevent relapse, it can be useful to recognize these circumstances and have backup plans ready.

Identifying your unique reason for wanting to stop smoking is essential to a successful quit attempt. Finding your own internal and external motivators will help you muster the courage and resolve to kick this harmful habit. It could mean the difference between a successful and unsuccessful attempt if you take the time to genuinely understand why quitting is vital.

Managing Triggers

Recognize your triggers to avoid giving in to the desire to pick up smokeless tobacco again because quitting can be very tough. The first week following your quit, these cravings will be at their peak in locations and circumstances where you used to chew or snuff. When managing triggers, the following information could be useful:

Make a list of potential trigger events and scenarios so you may prepare for them in advance.

Put down the actions you'll take in these circumstances to avoid smoking smokeless tobacco (such as chewing gum, cleaning your teeth, or just getting up and leaving the area).

Steer clear of alcohol as it may exacerbate use.

It takes a lot of work and perseverance to quit. If you do relapse, be kind to yourself. You can grow from your recurrence. In all that you do, NEVER GIVE UP! You're still trying to quit using smokeless tobacco. Although it may take several attempts to completely give up, the effort is worthwhile. There are numerous advantages to quitting, some of which you will experience immediately. You will experience a number of advantages and enhancements in the initial days after stopping smokeless tobacco, including Better breath—no more covering up the odor of tobacco with mints or gum!

Food will have a superior flavor.

Drugs to Aid with Your Quit

The difficulty of quitting smokeless tobacco "cold turkey" is well known to those who have attempted it. That being said, there are a number of drugs that might help you stop. Numerous of these drugs are also used to assist individuals in quitting smoking. For further information, see Medications.

Treatment with Nicotine Replacement (NRT)

With nicotine substitutes, you can get your fix without the other toxic components of tobacco. Among these goods are:

Nicotine gum is available without a prescription. Nicotine patches are available without a prescription. Nicotine lozenges are available without a prescription.

Nicotine inhaler: a prescription-only product.

Nicotine nasal spray: a prescription-only product.

While over-the-counter nicotine replacement therapy (NRT) treatments have few negative effects and may aid in quitting, the FDA has not approved the use of NRT to assist individuals in quitting smokeless tobacco. Nicotine gum or lozenges, which resemble smokeless tobacco the most, might be helpful if you like the sensation of anything in your mouth. Reduced nicotine withdrawal symptoms and tobacco cravings have been linked to 4 mg nicotine lozenges.

Helped Quit

The majority of smokers lack the necessary skills to abruptly quit.

Assisted cessation can help in this situation.

Cigarette Because nicotine is a highly addictive drug, withdrawal symptoms can be lessened using substitution therapy, which includes using nicotine patches, chewing gum, and other medications. Study up on the topic of nicotine replacement therapy.

Whichever route you ultimately decide on, you'll need a plan. The strategy you employ to control cravings, relapses, and withdrawal symptoms is known as your method. Here, there are lots of possibilities from which to select. The majority of them will be listed, along with any research that supports their efficacy.

Keep in mind that just because a given approach doesn't work for you doesn't imply there is another option that will work for you. Try out a few different strategies until you find one that works perfectly for you.

## The Quit Smoking Buddy System

It's difficult to stop when you're alone yourself. Try, if you can, to find a quit buddy who will commit to a healthy lifestyle and share your burden.

There are several advantages of using a buddy system to stop smoking:

You will be able to seek help when you need it and share your results with others. Supporting one another will be essential if one of you falters. In the event that you relapse, you will have someone to support you—or you them.

Recognize the influence of peer pressure in addition to the strength of unity. Research indicates that smokers who believe others would condemn them if they give up are nearly twice as likely to follow through on their promise to quit.

Competitions to Quit Smoking

There have been instances of businesses and campaigns successfully organizing competitions to stop smoking. It appears that external incentives like money and peer pressure are effective because studies have shown that smokers who enter a contest have twice the likelihood of quitting, even for 24 weeks.

You do not, however, need to hold out for a medical trial to come your way. Smokers typically hang out with other smokers, and you undoubtedly know people who also engage in this harmful behavior. Here's a little secret: you both want to overcome your addiction to nicotine. Start a competition among your friends and coworkers to stop smoking. A healthier life ought to be motivation enough, but you may spice things up with a bet. Set aside the amount of money you would typically spend on smokes, and the one who can stick with it for the full six months wins. The ideal result? With their own money in their pockets, each person leaves.

## Causes For Giving Up Smoking

Many smokers have given specific, well-defined reasons for wanting to give up; some wanted to quit for health-related reasons. This is not surprising, considering that over 400,000 Americans die each year from diseases brought on by smoking. Aspiratory emphysema, bronchitis, ulcers, heart problems, malignant growths, strokes, and peripheral vascular infections are a few of the more common illnesses that are directly caused by smoking.

Moreover, smoking may complicate the treatment of prior conditions. The risk of drowsiness and its effects on one's employability increase with cigarette use.

Another important reason to stop is the predominating burden. Nowadays, a large portion of the more than 50 million former smokers in our nation view smoking as disgusting, nauseating, and rotten. While smoking used to be seen as complicated, many of their friends and acquaintances now dislike those who smoke.

Currently, a few smokers feel that they lack the expertise to quit and that they are failing at self-control. A couple wants to stop smoking in order to provide a good example for their children.

Another noteworthy explanation is the expense associated with smoking. A lot of people remember saying, "If cigarettes ever get to $1.00 a pack, I'll quit!" As cigarettes are now costing many times that amount, the same number of people have continued to smoke. When a couple realizes they're spending a lot of money annually to support their addiction, they may be persuaded to give up smoking. Additionally, smokers eat holes in their clothes, cars, couches, and covers. Not only may costly purchases ensue, but unforeseen fires could also start. As a matter of fact, smoking cigarettes is the primary cause of nearly half of the fire deaths in our nation.

Many have resumed smoking after quitting for a crucial amount of time in the past. They felt healthier, more at ease, and happier after they were freed from smoking. Nevertheless, their lack of appreciation allowed them to lure a puff. This led to the acceptance of their complete compulsion.

Some people require help quitting smoking. They are aware of the dangers, suffering, and expense, but they are unable to stop. Smoking cigarettes is an addiction. The fundamental aspect of memorable is that once you become a fiend, you always remain a devil. Remaining off is not too difficult when you're quitting smoking for a short while. You'll occasionally think about smoking, but those thoughts pale in comparison to the cravings you felt during the early quitting phase.

But you should never forget that all it takes is one hit to put you back into a fully-fledged dependent state. At that time, you'll have to restart quitting smoking or find another way. Both of those are bad decisions. If you find yourself thinking about enjoying a drag, think about the two of them. Adhere to the leaders and never acknowledge another cigarette!

How I Started

I became an avid smoker at the age of eleven. I had never been to my friend's mother's place before. Since that's what kids in my generation did, we were just hanging out and talking while playing the Nintendo 64. He takes out a pack of cigarettes and lights one in front of me all of a sudden. I was unaware that he was a smoker.

Growing up, cigarettes were regarded as a bad thing in my household. I've always been independent and never really let other people influence me. Most of the time, I followed my own desires without giving my actions any thought to the consequences. However, I never saw myself smoking even back then. Regretfully, my friend was an excellent salesman.

"How did you get those?" I asked my friend as soon as I noticed him smoking a cigarette. "My mum bought them for me," he then revealed to me. It was unbelievable to me. "Why would his mum buy him cigarettes when he is the same age as me?" I began to wonder. I couldn't figure it out. "Why would you want to smoke, isn't it bad for you?" I asked him. "I have been smoking since I was nine years old, and I just enjoy the feeling of it," adds my friend.

I had to give it a try after my friend showed me how nice it felt and produced a few smoke rings. I took out a cigarette, inserted it into my mouth, and lighted it. I was on the verge of puking in my friend's kitchen sink as soon as the smoke entered my lungs and began to strike me violently. Surprisingly, after all that, I gave it another go, and this time, I kind of liked it.

I was interested after smoking my first cigarette and leaving my friend's house. Yes, at first, it made me cough, but after that, I felt OK. When adults warned me that smoking was extremely unhealthy, I didn't know what they were talking about. How can something cause you no pain even when it could be so harmful that you could die from it? Yes, the first puff hurt, but after that, it was fun.

I used to light up a couple of butts with the lighter my friend gave me on the way home. In case you're not aware, a cigarette butt is the part of a cigarette that someone discards after using it. I was curious to learn more about it. See why I like it despite how much it caused me to cough. My mind was racing with so many questions.

That is until my inquiries were all answered the following day. I woke up feeling quite sick. I believed I was going to pass away. Never in my entire life had I felt so ill. It felt like I had pneumonia again but with an unexplained discomfort in my lungs. I made a vow to never take up smoking ever again.

At thirteen, I picked up smoking cigarettes once more. The neighborhood library had become a hangout for all the disobedient kids. I met this 5-year-old kid there, and thereafter, going there was just a normal thing for me. You got used to the fact that this was a very small place. Maybe a pack a day was what I smoked at this point in my life. It was hardly a year long. When high school started, I gave up.

Stress was the reason I picked up smoking again after high school, and I enjoyed the sensation of smoke hitting my throat. I used to think that smoking was a great method to deal with stress. It was a great way for me to decompress and release tension. I would smoke one pack a day for years to come after this.

Simply give up.

Since it doesn't involve a third party to assist you, this is the most popular and ostensibly easiest method for quitting smoking. You essentially make an investment in abstaining from smoke. Although those who give up abruptly are more successful than those who do, just three to five percent of persons who give up abruptly manage to continue with it. Should you choose to forgo NRT, the process of abruptly stopping will be entirely dependent on your ability to exercise self-control.

Some people have a genetic advantage over others who can quit abruptly; 20% of people have a genetic change that lessens the pleasant effects of nicotine.

To increase your chances of success when quitting suddenly, try substituting new activities for smoking.

If you are unable to give up immediately, think about using a reinforcement approach.

Although it is the easiest system to use, it is also the most difficult to finish successfully.

Try a nicotine replacement therapy program.

With a 20% success rate, NRT is among the greatest tools for treating smoking habits. You can provide the nicotine their bodies need by biting gum, swallowing pills, or using patches. Over time, you can gradually reduce the dosage and wean them off of nicotine. You will gradually move away from behavior that becomes a habit and towards constructive endeavors.

If you decide to stop smoking immediately and begin using NRTs instead of gradually cutting back on your cigarette use, you will undoubtedly cease. In one research, just 15.5% of smokers who consistently cut back north of roughly fourteen days were abstinent after a half-year, compared to 22% of new smokers.

You can usually get nicotine gum, patches, and tablets at your local pharmacy without a prescription.

Purchases of gum, patches, or capsules are necessary for this operation, which will cost money.

Treatment with nicotine swapping is less successful in those whose digestive systems assimilate nicotine quickly. Discuss your digestive issues and the nicotine replacement treatment with your physician.

Business

Obtain medicine to help you quit. Medication designed to help you regulate your cravings, such as varenicline (Chantix) and bupropion (Zyban, Wellbutrin), can be recommended by your PCP. Discuss the side effects of these medications and whether they are right for you with your doctor.

It has been demonstrated that bupropion completely alters the viability of smoking cessation programs for those with fast nicotine metabolism.

Verify that your solution plan covers these medications by contacting your insurance provider.

Proceed to counselling or therapy.

Collaborate with an advisor or expert to address the underlying, very personal issues that underlie your smoking. This can help you identify the situational or close-to-home triggers that make you want to smoke

Find out if your well-being plan includes directing by contacting your protection provider.

Before attempting any initiatives or techniques related to smoking cessation, make sure you are completely ready to quit. When trying to control a dependency, you should put yourself in a positive state of mind, not one of disappointment. Guiding can be a very helpful tool for identifying the barriers preventing you from giving up.[9]

Examine the procedures of electives.

There are lots of different optional activities that can help you give up smoking. These range from mineral and herbal supplements to hypnotic exercises like meditation. While some smokers have found success with these methods, there isn't any rational evidence to back them up.

Many smokers consume vitamin C candies and pills, which they acknowledge help them manage their cravings.

Thinking about it can be a useful technique to help refocus your mind from the need to smoke.

Employ a variety of approaches.

Even while you might find that one strategy helps you quit, you might need to use other strategies to continue not smoking. It's possible that your fundamental approach is irrational and requires you to employ reinforcement, or you may find that using two strategies at once to address your wants is easier.

Speak with your doctor to make sure you are not taking your medications together in an unfavorable way.

Consider using an elective method with a more standardized process.

## Measures Implemented By The Iron Hands Of The Government

As more and more people in the upper classes have become aware of the long-term repercussions of smoking, the government has started to take action against this feared epidemic. With the exception of mesothelioma, most cancer types have been related to smoking.

Different governments have launched a number of efforts, including some symbolic ones like the Non-smoking Day. At the summit, the subject was even brought up at the highest level of discourse, and shared platforms were also suggested. It would be foolish to ignore the issue; instead, people from all walks of life have started to educate smokers—including the younger generation—about the dangers of this deadly addiction.

This is the point at which consciousness reaches. International cricket competitions are no longer sponsored by ITC, the renowned cigarette brand. Worldwide, most public areas are smoke-free; long-haul trains strictly prohibit smoking; and most restaurants and entertainment venues have made smoking non-permissible. Remember that smoking affects not just the smoker but also their friends, family, and especially the children who bear the burden of bearing the future of humanity. We'd like to highlight some of the most significant declarations and initiatives from governments throughout the globe in favour of the anti-smoking campaign in this post.

American endeavors

A last-ditch effort to reduce tobacco use is being made by federal, state, local, and health organizations. These efforts are centered on mass and speedy outcomes.

Restricting youth access to tobacco in order to stop them from ever lighting up.

● Changes to the healthcare system that support smoking cessation may result in a decrease in the average number of cigarettes consumed annually. Both Massachusetts and California increased their cigarette excise taxes while setting aside a specific sum of money for tobacco control programs.

● Education programs teach school-age youngsters the value of staying away from the start and finish of top-notch health education curriculum at the grade level. Comprehensive knowledge of smoking cessation methods and a solid comprehension of the harmful effects of tobacco use. ● helping tobacco users give up in order to reduce the risk that dense smoke will enter the lungs of those who are not smokers.

Effective evaluation techniques for monitoring program outcomes result in the use of earlier iterations to create newer, more powerful versions of the programs that were implemented. Treatment for nicotine addiction aids in recovery and helps individuals rediscover their purpose in life. School-based tobacco prevention initiatives identify the social factors that promote youth tobacco use and impart information on how to avoid them. These therapies have consistently and significantly reduced or delayed the rate of adolescent smoking.

Let's examine a few strategies that people have used to break their relationship with cigarettes.

Numerous smoking cessation strategies have been floated around in books, magazines, and chat shows on television throughout the years. Typically, they lacked scientific or medical validity. While not all of these recommendations are sound, and the majority are ineffective, it's interesting to see what has been tried throughout the years.

Take advantage of being sick with the flu or a nasty cold to stop.

Smoke is a heavier brand or a flavor that you find objectionable.

Packs of cigarettes should be wrapped like presents so that you have to open them to acquire the smoke.

To get tired of cigarettes, smoke ten times as much each day.

List the items you wish to purchase, along with their prices. Determine the cost of packs of cigarettes. It will force you to cut costs.

Give the key to a stranger and lock your packs inside a safe.

When you have the need, take a shower.

Choose to limit your smoking to odd or even numbers of hours.

Determine the total cost of smokes for a year. Purchase a money order for that sum, then give it to a companion. They get paid if you smoke in that particular year.

I will discuss with you some of the tried-and-true smoking cessation strategies that millions of ex-smokers have used in the book's upcoming chapters. I'm hoping they're useful.

And in case you require additional motivation to choose not to smoke:

Consider how much a single pack of smokes costs. Divide that amount by the total number of packs you smoke each month. 30 or 60 years old? If you had that money, what would be the extent of your options?

Think about how long it takes to stop at a petrol station and pick up another pack. Extra breaks that result in non-productive time at the job.Looking around the house for that dang hard-to-find lighter.

Your life will be under your control. You can stop worrying about when you can run outdoors to light up and where the next pack is.

Protecting your loved ones from secondhand smoke. They could develop cancer even if they never started. You want to avoid being the reason behind that.

Breathing while doing physical activity. You'll be able to keep up your current weight and possibly even drop a little.

When you're short on cash because you bought another box of smokes, your pals will appreciate that you didn't ask them for money.

Strangers will no longer give you odd looks when you're out in public.

The premiums for your life insurance won't be too high.

Right here, make your own list of reasons to give up. I've given you a few to get you going. Make use of the advice provided in the earlier chapters. And then use your personal experiences to develop your own.

Giving up smoking will enable me to have the following:

brighter teeth

more pristine breath

More cash

You can now move forward in life.

Once you have successfully quit smoking, you should take urgent action to eliminate the habit's aftereffects.

Make sure your carpet is clean.

Together with the upholstery and your drapery.

If your clothing smells like smoke, wash it.

Brush your teeth and wash your hair.

Get rid of all ashtrays.

Throw away the empty pop cans, bottles, Styrofoam containers, and any other materials you used to hold the ashes.

Give your lighters away.

Use scented candles or air fresheners.

Additionally, make it clear to everyone who enters your home that smoking is no longer permitted.

## The Effects Of Nicotine On The Body

Nicotine and other artificial substances found in cigarette smoke are effectively absorbed by the lungs. Nicotine then quickly permeates the entire body.

When modest amounts of nicotine are used, they provide pleasant feelings and distract the user from unpleasant ones. This increases the client's craving for tobacco use. It is founded on the study of the concentrated sensory system and the mind, and it has an impact on temperament. Nicotine acts by overstimulating the brain's dopaminergic reward circuits, just like other seductive substances do. Additionally, a small adrenaline spike brought on by nicotine increases heart rate and pulse but does not cause a visual impairment.

Nicotine enters the bloodstream shortly after smoking and takes a few minutes to wear off. The client can get anxious and upset. Most of the time, it doesn't get bad enough to cause obvious withdrawal symptoms, but eventually, the user starts to feel uneasy. This often encourages the person to achieve enlightenment again. When the terrible emotions eventually pass, and the person picks up smoking once more, the pattern repeats itself. If, as is rare, the person does not immediately resume smoking, the withdrawal symptoms gradually go away.

Smokers typically increase their cigarette usage as their bodies adjust to the nicotine. They, therefore, have elevated blood nicotine levels, and it is thought that smoking more tobacco will have a potent effect.

We refer to this as resistance. The user needs to keep using the product consistently to keep the level of nicotine within a comfortable range after they have gradually achieved a certain level.

When someone stops smoking, they could rapidly develop a nicotine addiction and suffer negative physiological effects. These adverse effects include headaches, irritability, anxiety, and trouble falling asleep. The actual form of slavery negatively impacts people's quality of life, well-being, and familial relationships.

You might also wish to stop using these recommendations.

Write it down as follows: People who have written objectives tend to achieve greater success than those who don't.

List all the advantages of stopping smoking, such as the money you'll save or the extra energy you'll have for physical activity. Make sure the list is always accessible. Add the others as you think of them.

Get assistance. Support from friends and family increases the likelihood that they will be successful in stopping it. If you don't want to tell your family that you smoke, ask your friends to help you quit.

Jitteriness, melancholy, or irritability.

Absence of energy

a painful throat or dry mouth

a hunger pang.

Have patience; the effects of quitting nicotine will subside. The impulse to sneak a smoke can worsen the withdrawal symptoms, so try to resist it.

Don't stray from your plan. Many people find that because they have work or school on Mondays, it's simpler to quit then. The more preoccupied you are, the less likely it is that you will want to smoke. Exercise not only serves as a good diversion but also maintains your energy levels and weight under control.

Stop gradually. Some people find that progressively reducing their daily cigarette intake is a successful way to stop smoking. However, not everyone can profit from this strategy. You could find that it's better for you to give up smoking "cold turkey" and suddenly.

If necessary, think about using a nicotine replacement. If none of these strategies work for you, talk to your doctor about prescription drugs such as nicotine replacement gums, patches, inhalers, or nasal sprays. Sprays and inhalers can only be purchased by people with a prescription. That's why it's so important to visit your doctor before buying the gum and patch off the shelf. The effects of various therapies vary (for instance, while the patch is simple to use, other treatments provide a quicker hit of nicotine). Your doctor can help you decide what the best course of action is for you.

Mistakes Do Occur: If you make a mistake, don't give up! False starts to significant changes are common. Like many others, you may be able to effectively quit smoking for weeks or even months at a time before an overwhelming temptation compels you to give in. Or perhaps you inadvertently find yourself in one of your trigger situations and give in to temptation.

You haven't failed if you make a mistake. That's all—you're still a human. The following three tactics will help you get back on track:

Think of your mistake as a single mistake. After noting the event and cause, continue.

Did one cigarette lead to heavy smoking for you? Probably not. It has happened more gradually over time. It won't make you a smoker again, just as smoking one cigarette—or even two or three—after giving up didn't make you one in the first place.

Ask a friend, family member, or support system to remind you of your achievements and the reasons you decided to stop, or you can do it yourself.

Reward yourself. Quitting smoking is not easy. Treat yourself to something you merit! Set aside the money you usually spend on smokes. If you've been smoke-free for one, two, or three weeks, treat yourself to something nice, like a movie ticket, gift card, or new clothes. A year without smoking is something to be happy about. You're worthy of it.

## Why Give Up Smoking?

And there is ample evidence of the negative health effects of smoking. There are several risks associated with smoking; thus, one of the most crucial things you can do to enhance your health and quality of life is to give up smoking. We'll look at the several reasons why giving up smoking is so important for your health in this chapter.

Decreased Chance of Severe Health Issues

In addition to respiratory diseases like emphysema and chronic bronchitis, These illnesses may be deadly, extremely costly to treat, and severely incapacitating. Giving up smoking can lower your chance of getting these illnesses dramatically and, in certain situations, even undo some of the harm that smoking has done to your body.

Better Health of the Respiratory System

Smoking harms the lungs by decreasing lung function and producing inflammation in the respiratory system. Breathing difficulties, a persistent cough, and other respiratory issues may result from this injury. Giving up smoking can enhance lung function and respiratory health by lowering symptoms.

Improved Heart Health


Better Mental Health: Smoking is frequently used as a stress and anxiety coping method. Smoking, however, can exacerbate anxiety and worsen mental health conditions. Giving up smoking has been shown to enhance mental health by lowering anxiety and elevating mood.

## Economic Advantages

Smoking is a costly habit since cigarettes may get pricey over time. You can save a lot of money by giving up smoking, which you can use for other enjoyable activities.

## Enhanced Life Quality

Smoking can significantly lower one's quality of life by impairing one's vitality, ability to exercise, and general well-being. Giving up smoking can enhance your life by giving you more energy and enabling you to participate in things you would not have enjoyed while smoking.

## Alternative Medical Interventions

There are a few methods for quitting smoking that don't include vaping, nicotine replacement therapy, or prescription medications. Among them are:

Spellbinding: For some smokers trying to quit, this well-known option has had excellent results. Ignore everything you've seen on stage, hypnotists; spellbinding operates by putting you in a deeply relaxed state where you're open to suggestions that strengthen your resolve to stop smoking and heighten your negative feelings towards cigarettes.

Needle therapy is one of the most well-known and proven clinical techniques. Needlestring treatment can be helpful in managing the negative effects of smoking cessation.

Conduct Therapy: Regular smoking-related behaviors and rituals are linked to nicotine dependency. The goal of conduct treatment is to overcome those inclinations and develop new adaptive skills.

Inspirational Therapies: Self-help books and canning websites offer different strategies to motivate yourself to give up smoking entirely. Calculating the money associated with investment funds is one prominent model. For some people, the opportunity to find the motivation to quit has been provided by calculating their savings. It could very well be enough to cover the cost of a late-spring getaway.

Spit or smokeless tobacco is unquestionably not a good substitute for smoking.

In contrast to smoking cigarettes, using smokeless tobacco, often known as spit or biting tobacco, is undoubtedly not a safe choice. It has nicotine, a substance that is comparable to that found in cigarettes. In actuality, the amount of nicotine that is retained from smokeless tobacco can range from three to several times that of cigarettes.

What to Do If You Fall Or Relapse

It's common for people to make multiple attempts at quitting smoking before giving up the habit permanently, so don't beat yourself up if you make a mistake and light up. If everything else is equal, turn the autumn into a springboard by learning from your mistakes.

Analyze what transpired before you started smoking again, identify any triggers or trouble spots you encountered, and create a new quitting plan that addresses them.

Stressing the differences between a slip and a relapse is also important. Even if you start smoking again, that doesn't mean you can't get back in the cart. You have two options: either you learn from the slip and let it motivate you to work harder, or you assign blame in an attempt to get back into your smoking habit. That being said, the choice is entirely yours. It's not necessary for a slip to turn into a complete collapse. In the unlikely event that you make a mistake, you won't let anyone down. It doesn't mean you have to give up completely.

Make an effort to prevent a slip from becoming a landslip. Throw away the rest of the pack. It is imperative that you return to your non-smoking path immediately. Review your quit journal and feel happy about the period of time you spent quitting.

Consider as the catalyst. And why specifically did you feel the need to smoke again? Decide how you will handle that situation the next time it arises.

Make use of your expertise. What has proven to be generally beneficial? What failed to work?

Do you really believe that you are using medicine to help you quit? In the unlikely event that you start smoking again, give your PCP a call. Taking certain medications at the same time that you smoke is not recommended.

# Easy Methods For Giving Up Smoking

To stop smoking and manage your nicotine cravings, use these strategies.
Acupuncture: While smoking cigarettes can help you relax, the negative side effects outweigh the relaxation. Acupuncture has a sedative effect on the nervous system, which lessens withdrawal symptoms and cravings for nicotine. Additionally, receiving acupuncture treatment raises blood levels of beta-endorphins and reduces the desire for nicotine. Your desire for nicotine will be lessened by acupuncture, but it won't make you stop smoking. You alone have the ability to quit smoking, which is why willpower is so important. The symptoms of nicotine withdrawal, including jitters, restlessness, and irritability, are lessened by acupuncture. Typically, you will require two treatments in the second week and three treatments in the

first. After one month, you might require a few follow-up treatments if your nicotine addiction is severe. Tar and nicotine residue are among the harmful substances that acupuncture also purges your blood of.

Hypnosis: Research has indicated that hypnosis is beneficial for chain smokers; it's not just the typical method you've seen on TV. Hypnotists with advanced degrees from reputable universities practice at rehab and treatment facilities that are reliable. The cost of hypnosis can range from $80 to $200 per hour. For noticeable improvement, you might require one to four hypnosis sessions, depending on the severity of your nicotine addiction. Typically, deep, calm breathing, visualization, and relaxation precede hypnosis. A skilled hypnotist can help a patient go from a worried and negative state of mind to one of hyperresponsiveness and gradually replace it with positive and healthy thoughts. A well-known name in the field of hypnosis is, According to Dr. John McGrail, "The subconscious mind of a patient is viewed by hypnosis as a computer hard disc, which replaces old, out-of-date software with new software." Although hypnosis usually works for everyone, it is not a miracle cure. The patient's willpower is crucial. Hypnosis won't be able to cure nicotine addiction unless the smoker is committed to giving up. Consult a reputable hypnotist to ensure a full recovery.

Electronic cigarettes: A recent study that was published in "The Cochrane Library" claims that smokers who use e-cigarettes to quit have successfully reduced their smoking or given up entirely. According to the study, one in ten smokers was able to completely stop, and one in three smokers was able to cut their smoking requirement in half. Co-author of the study, Professor Peter Hajek, advises chain smokers who have not been successful with nicotine patches to switch to e-cigarettes for improved outcomes. Despite evidence that regular smokers have used e-cigarettes to successfully quit, the FDA has not yet approved e-cigarettes. When purchasing e-cigarettes, be cautious, as some of them contain nicotine.

Meditation: Using meditation techniques to stop smoking. According to a University of Wisconsin study, 60% of chain smokers who also meditate have been able to successfully stop smoking. As you go through the withdrawal process, regular meditation will help you control your negative thoughts and feelings, reduce stress, and lessen your craving for nicotine. Meditation can be very beneficial and effective. By strengthening your mind through meditation, you can better manage smoking triggers and better control your craving for nicotine. Your health will greatly benefit from meditation, and there are no additional costs or negative effects.

Diet to stop smoking: Maintaining a smoke-free lifestyle depends greatly on your diet. Before smoking, consume milk or fresh fruit and vegetables like carrots and celery. You will experience a bitter aftertaste when you smoke a cigarette after consuming these foods and beverages. To reduce your craving for nicotine, eat fruits high in vitamin C, such as guava, lemon, and organs. Nicotine makes you dependent on it by filling in the vitamin C deficiency. Thus, if you get enough vitamin C, you'll eventually feel less of a craving for nicotine. Eat some pickles or salty snacks like chips whenever you get the urge to smoke. Dried fruit aromas will help you suppress your cravings. Eat some candy or chew gum to keep your mouth occupied. Steer clear of red meat, alcohol, and caffeine excess, as these can exacerbate cravings for nicotine.

## What Makes Smoking So Enjoyable For Smokers?

Smoking can be a comforting and pleasurable activity for many people. Smoking is a complicated behavior that many smokers find enjoyable for a variety of reasons.

Among the most popular explanations for why people enjoy smoking are as follows:

1 The Nicotine High: When smoked, nicotine, a highly addictive drug, gives users a pleasant high. This sensation, which is frequently characterized as a calming influence or a release of tension, can offer momentary relief from depression, anxiety, and stress.

2 The Ritual: Smoking is a ritual that provides solace and enjoyment for certain smokers. Eating can be a repetitive, soothing activity for smokers, from choosing their brand to holding and puffing.

3 The Perception of Coolness: Smoking is connected to a certain degree of style and sophistication for some smokers. For many people, smoking is seen as a means of projecting an image of independence and confidence. This perception of smoking as "cool" has been

reinforced by popular culture and advertising for decades.

4 The Feeling of Community: Smoking is a social activity that many people enjoy doing with friends and family. Smoking together, whether during a social gathering or while taking a break, can foster a sense of camaraderie and community.

5 The Habit: Smoking has become a difficult habit for some smokers to break. Smoking has the potential to become a deeply ingrained habit that brings comfort and pleasure through its rituals and repetitive behaviors.

It's crucial to remember that smoking is a dangerous and fatal habit despite the apparent pleasure it brings.

Consequently, even though smoking might bring about momentary comfort and pleasure, it's important to understand that smoking has far worse long-term effects than any momentary advantages. The best way to enjoy a longer, healthier life and lower your risk of serious health problems is to give up smoking.

# Behavioural Techniques And Reversing Habits

By recognizing our triggers and adopting healthy coping mechanisms for cravings, we are able to kick the smoking habit.

## Section 1: Recognising Your Smoking Habit and Its Triggers

### 1.1 Recognising the Part Habits Play in Addiction to Smoking

Nicotine dependence, as well as the customs and habits related to smoking, are the main causes of smoking addiction. Achieving a successful smoking cessation requires breaking these habits. By recognizing the triggers that lead to smoking and substituting them with healthier options, you can overcome the smoking habit.

### 1.2 Identifying High-Risk Events and Triggers

Events, feelings, or circumstances known as triggers increase your likelihood of reaching for a cigarette. Stress, get-togethers, places, or even particular activities. You can better navigate high-risk situations and create coping mechanisms to avoid or manage them without smoking by identifying your triggers.

1.3 Establishing a Smoke-Free Ambience

Establishing a supportive atmosphere is essential to helping people stop smoking. Clear your surroundings of any items related to smoking, like lighters and ashtrays. To get rid of the smoke smell in your living areas, clean and freshen them up.

Section 2: Methods for Controlling Cravings and Giving Up Smoking Habits

2.1 Methods of Behavioural Replacement

Making healthier substitutions for smoking habits is one successful quitting technique. If you smoke, for instance, give up the habit and replace it with something else, like going for a quick walk or practicing deep breathing. You can intentionally break the connection between particular activities and smoking by substituting constructive behaviors for smoking.

## 2.2 Strategies for Diversion

Strong cravings can be difficult to resist. You can help yourself by using techniques of distraction to take your mind off of thoughts and desires related to smoking. Take up hand and mind-occupying hobbies like knitting, puzzles, reading, or playing an instrument. To help you relax and resist the cravings, try deep breathing exercises or mindfulness training.

## 2.3 Accountability and Support Systems

Having a network of support can greatly improve your attempts to stop smoking. Seek out the assistance of loved ones, friends, or support groups who can offer encouragement when cravings or difficulties emerge and who are aware of your journey. Think about finding a quiet partner with whom you can discuss your progress, obstacles, and victories. Having someone else hold you accountable can boost your motivation and keep you on course.

2.4 Incentives

Giving yourself a reward for reaching milestones and succeeding in quitting can be very inspiring. Achieve attainable objectives, like quitting smoking for a week or hitting a certain month-end milestone, and treat yourself to something enjoyable, like a massage, a special treat, or a small purchase, as a reward. Honoring your accomplishments motivates you to stay smoke-free by reinforcing good behavior.

In conclusion, behavioral tactics and habit-reversal methods are essential for successful smoking cessation. By recognizing your triggers, quitting smoking, and substituting healthier behaviors for smoking, you can establish new patterns and associations that support your smoke-free lifestyle. To maintain motivation and focus, use strategies for diversion, enlist the aid of others, and set up a system of rewards. Recall that giving up smoking is a process that calls for endurance, self-compassion, and patience. We'll give you more advice and resources to help you stick to your smoke-free lifestyle and succeed in your quest for ideal health.

## Light Up And Prepare To Pay The Penalty

Smoke from cigarettes, in any amount, is harmful to your health. It's astonishing that the only things that are promoted as causing cancer are cigarettes. It is utterly false to say that smoking fewer filtered cigarettes has no negative effects.

A person's risk of injury and early death increases when they smoke one to four cigarettes each day.

The hazards are the same whether a person smokes a high-tar, low-tar, high-nicotine, or low-nicotine brand. Additionally, excessive cigarette smoking is caused by the idea that safer alternatives exist. The same injury is still done to the individual.

ultimately develops deeper, more frequent puffs and a shorter butt. As a result, the addictive drug's amount of intoxicating nicotine remains constant. Studies show that smokers do not have a decreased risk of lung cancer if they smoke less tar or nicotine. Tiny amounts of nicotine damage the brain and central nervous system, producing pleasurable feelings that influence the smoker's mood and enhance his urge to smoke.

Because of this, when someone tries to kick their almost deadly, dangerous habits, they have physical withdrawal symptoms.

Out of bounds for the next generation

Limiting minors' access to tobacco products is a primary controlling factor in the multifaceted approach aimed at decreasing tobacco consumption.

● In order to stop students or teenagers from buying cigarettes or other tobacco products, age verification will be required. Personal self-care: Because tobacco displays made it simpler for kids to buy or steal tobacco goods, they were removed.

But, due to the shameful lack of enforcement of these laws, numerous malpractices have been harming vulnerable saplings before the strict measures to keep minors away have even been put in place.

- Towns have turned to enforcement actions, retailer education, and compliance inspections. Most states forbid the use of cigarette vending machines, with the exception of those where kids are unable to use them. All States must revoke licenses for access laws that affect the main strategy used to try to prevent minors from acquiring tobacco products in order to meet the aims of federal policy. Their campaign should center on the social networks that young people use—such as their parents, siblings, and friends—to make cigarette purchases.

- Teenagers' perceptions of the following elements increase their likelihood of smoking tobacco:

1. Tobacco use is the norm because their siblings and peers support them in using tobacco products.

2. The unwavering conviction that it greatly enhances mental clarity, which boosts morale in stressful situations.

3. The health risks associated with using chewing tobacco are usually too complex for developing brains to understand.

It's possible to quit smoking in an hour.

After you had your first cigarette, did you ever think it was not that bad? Maybe you're still trying to kick the habit after all these years, lighting up a cigarette while you look into other options.

Your best option might be to use medications that are intended to ease withdrawal symptoms and facilitate the quitting process if you're looking for a way to stop smoking in an hour. In just one hour, these pills can assist you in giving up smoking. These products, which include nicotine gum, patches, and lozenges, can be bought over-the-counter (OTC) at pharmacies across the country. Many people turn to these products as an easier way to quit smoking but don't want to see a doctor; just watch out that you don't take more than the suggested amount.

You've undoubtedly already tried a number of strategies if you're trying to quit smoking, such as setting up several dates to quit, buying nicotine patches or e-cigarettes to help with the withdrawal symptoms, or just giving up cold turkey. However, if you haven't been able to stop smoking yet, it might not be your fault—it's possible that you just aren't aware of how to stop smoking in an hour! You're in luck because this post will guide you through every step of permanently stopping smoking, allowing you to live a tobacco-free, healthy life without experiencing the uncomfortable symptoms of nicotine withdrawal.

Although quitting smoking is often thought to be one of the hardest habits to break, all it takes is understanding how to stop smoking in just one hour. You'll discover how easy it is to stop smoking by following these five steps if you adhere to this guide.

If you smoke, you've probably made multiple attempts to stop smoking, but like most smokers, you were never able to make it past the first day. If you want to stop smoking in an hour, you should take the advice of the many smokers who have done so successfully and apply it to your own plan of action. You should take advice from the many smokers who have successfully quit in less than an hour if your goal is to stop smoking in just that much time. If you follow the instructions in this article, you should be able to quit smoking in an hour with very little cravings and very little withdrawal symptoms.

With the right knowledge, quitting smoking is doable in just one hour. You'll be smoke-free in no time at all if you just follow these easy steps!

You are itching for some clean, fresh air again because you can no longer stand the stale smell of smoke. You want to give up smoking for good, regardless of how long it has been since you last smoked—it could have been a day or many years. How on earth can you do that is the question. It may seem unachievable to quit smoking when you think back to how many times you've tried in the past. But what if I told you there was a methodical approach that would ensure you were able to stop smoking in just one hour? Would you be willing to learn more about it? You're correct on that!

It's normal to feel motivated to stop smoking after learning about the dangers of tobacco use and secondhand smoke, the price of cigarettes, and how strongly smoking odors your breath and clothes. For a brief moment, though, consider that you could break the habit in an hour. It seems too wonderful to be true, yet that's not the case at all! The first step to cold turkey quitting or gradually reducing your smoking habit is admitting you have a problem. If your tobacco addiction makes you feel as though you are stuck with it, don't panic; you don't have to.

If you have ever attempted to quit smoking, you are aware of the difficulties in doing so and continuing to live a life devoid of tobacco usage. However, there are successful people, and you may be one of them. You can virtually instantly overcome your addiction to cigarettes, cigars, and chewing tobacco via hypnosis. Hypnosis can also help you cope with the emotional triggers that may have initially led to the development of your addiction when used in conjunction with a treatment plan created by a qualified practitioner. Let's discover how hypnosis can help you stop smoking in just one hour.

Although smoking is not an easy task, it can be made easier with the right strategy. [B lah, blah] As long as the individual trying to quit has access to the right tools and knowledge, there are effective ways to stop smoking in as little as one hour. [blah blah]. The operation is as follows...

Not only is cigarette smoking terrible for your physical health, but it's critical to have a strategy in place to help you deal with the psychological implications of your decision. Your relatives and friends who support your decision to give up smoking permanently will also find it easier to adjust if you do this. It's critical to have a strategy in place before you stop smoking in order to manage the psychological repercussions of stopping. Decide on a quit date.

www.ingramcontent.com/pod-product-compliance
Lightning Source LLC
Chambersburg PA
CBHW052143110526
44591CB00012B/1838